Out of place

Kevin Holloway

With best wishes and love
~ and for much valued
support over time ~
Kevin

for
Mat and Lol,
of course

Published by Half Moon Books 2019
an imprint of OWF Press Community Interest Company
Otley Courthouse
www.owfpress.com

ISBN 978-1-9993036-5-5

Cover design: Nick Palmer

Acknowledgements

Croig Harbour was published in Strix magazine, issue 5. Versions of *Starlings* and *Curlew* won the first and runner-up prizes in the Saltaire Writers Group poetry competition 2018 and were published on the Saltaire Writers Group blog. *Stepping Stones* was published in Suburban Magazine, Leeds – edition 36.

I'd like to thank all involved with the Otley Courthouse Writers for their kind and thoughtful support for my writing, and my thanks also to members of Otley Poets and the Otley Stanza for such good advice and encouragement.

Printed & bound by ImprintDigital.com, UK

Contents

Defining terms

It doesn't always take a professor
of an ology to get to the core
of something, to cut through confusion
with such pleasing rightness it feels like when
an axe hits and splits a log exactly
down its middle, or when a bendy plastic
spatula drags up every last drop
of icing from the bowl in one long wipe,
or like when I first settled in the north
and, confused by new words, I asked next door
how a ginnel differed from a snicket:
That's easy lad, my neighbour said, *you'll*
stop a dog with yer legs in a snicket
but yuv no chance at all in a ginnel.

Saving Gotham

Standing up there all day,
high on the towers of the civic hall,
a pair of three metre tall golden owls,
watching over English Gotham.

Wouldn't that be grand,
two guardians of the city,
leaving their perches at night,
and, like the caped crusader,
saving us from incompetence and danger:
huge curved talons snatching
drowning drunkards from the river,
muggers lifted up mid-robbery,
missing youngsters flown home
lying on a giant feathered back.

Sometimes, walking by
in the early hours, I've looked up
and hoped to see the towers empty.
But no, the owls are always there,
motionless and lifeless in the darkness,
gold reflecting the city's orange glow;
I suspect we're in this on our own.

Sacred ground

The small wall by the offices
had lost a brick, exposing
its hollow neighbour,
all squarely defined inside,
tiny terracotta cells
arranged like office pigeon holes.

Every cell contained an old fag butt,
three neat rows of tribute
to the lips that held them,
that pursed tight, pulled smoke,
left lipstick, coffee, red bull,
a touch of early whisky on them.

Lips that kissed that morning,
snogged, crescent mooned a spoon,
smiled, spat, whistled for a dog,
cursed another driver, felt front teeth
fierce with Anglo-Saxon, said:
love you, don't forget the kids.

Lips that made a tight thin slit,
shaped smoke as fingers stubbed the butt,
placed it in a cell with care,
I was here, I made this, I am,
like tatters hung in trees
in olden times, and now.

A way with bones

So what of Peter, the city market fishmonger,
fingers numb among the shoals of fish
and squid and twitching crabs and ice,
sharpening his knife for filleting,
gentle touch finding every bone?
What is his role and contribution?

It may be slight for those knowing their own mind:
the wrapping round some smokey Craster kippers,
bagging up a weighty swiezy Karp.
But for anyone uncertain Peter has advice.
Watch him question, listen, ask:
What kind of meal? Who are you cooking for?

And watch him hear beneath their words, reach
below the skin, touch the bones of who they are
and finding need, meet it in his own sweet way.
For the hot and fevered he might offer
Arctic Halibut, for those struggling
with cold, golden south Indian Ruhoo.

He goes deeper: for those he finds subdued
he'll suggest a Headless Red, to shoppers
on the manic side he'll offer Monkfish tail,
when he sees timidity he'll indicate
a piece of big mouthed Snapper,
for someone overbearing a delicate Dorade.

Peter spends his days in conversation;
where he hears depression he'll recommend
fresh Cod-fish wings, if change is needed, Octopus.
He gives no reasons, simply makes suggestions,
but old customers return and he continues,
offering his time, his subtle way with bones.

The 23rd Mall

Our latest development is a new shopping and leisure centre on the edge of the city.

The Mall is my storehouse,
I shall not want.

It opened in 2013 with over 140 000 visitors on opening day.

It maketh me to park in zoned parking,
it leadeth me besides the cool products.

The new development has a catchment area of over 6.5 million people.

It restoreth my soul, it taketh my debts
and consolidateth them for its name's sake.

This population offers a potential retail spend of nearly 4 billion pounds annually.

Yea, though I walk through the valley
of the shadow of debt, I will fear no evil,
for thy credit is with me,
my card and my cash they comfort me.

Our new location has over 1 000 000 square feet of floor space and 130 shops, all anchored by new flagship stores for major national chains.

Thou preparest a counter before me
in the presence of my creditors,
thou anointest me with offers,
my cup runneth over.

A 30 000 square foot glass dome crowns the new mall with its 2000 glass panels rising a spectacular 140 feet above street level.

Surely money and feel-good shall
follow me all the days of my life.

The mall has a dedicated food area with a range of dining experiences offered. Accommodation with major hotel groups is available nearby.

And I will dwell in the shops of the Mall
for ever.

Note: Acknowledging various versions of Psalm 23 and Wikipedia entries on shopping malls.

Prey

There were two wings
lying where the city
pavement met a shop front,

a pair of pigeon wings, as if
a pigeon had lain down on
its back and had its body taken.

Two small perfect angel wings.
But nothing else explaining
why the wings were there,

no remains or bloodied
feathers, no rotting carcass
to indicate disease or injury.

Sparrowhawk, said Steph and
gestured upwards, *there'll be one*
here with all these birds around.

Beaks like knives, they'll
slice a kill apart in seconds,
bloody feathers everywhere.

My minds eye saw a small
soft body being butchered
on a parapet above me,

discarded blue-grey wings
    blown free to drift and fall,
        litter, tumbled on the breeze.

I stared down at the wings,
    sensed a hawk perched
        high above, inspecting.

Walking on I felt unease,
    conscious of a cold intent
        measuring its prey.

The girl who became a kitchen

She put on her house coat and demonstrated its utility:
the drop down chopping board supported at waist height
by two wooden fold out brackets;
the velcro fastened pockets down each arm holding
knives, whisks, spoons and other implements;
the small insulated boxes for perishables
attached by carabiners to the belt loops of her coat.
It's because I want to travel, she said by way of
explanation, and added, *I may need a kitchen where I'm going.*

I didn't doubt she might need a kitchen on her journey,
but the provision she'd made for never being far from one
surprised me.
And cooking? I asked. She took a small folding stove
from one side pocket of the coat and a little pan from
another. She placed them on the wooden chopping board
and looked at me triumphantly.
Well, you've really thought of everything, I said.
I hope so, she replied.

She sighed a little and took on the pensive frown
and burdened posture of one who, having aimed so high,
now senses that a task may be beyond them.
I wanted to offer something, give encouragement.
You'll have fun at parties, I said.
She looked at me, quizzically.
Well, you know where people always congregate at parties?
She laughed and set to, packing up her stove, and pan,
and drop-down wooden chopping board.

Two roe deer

I looked up while walking and saw two deer
in undergrowth just ten yards away,
a doe and a young buck in its first year.

They were side by side, both heads turned around
together, staring, as if straight at me.
I wondered why they'd held their ground

until I saw they were upwind of my scent,
and as I was camouflaged by dappled
shade they'd stayed, alert but confident.

I watched in shallow-breathing quiet:
the rounded barrel of the doe's torso,
the buck's first antlers sheathed in velvet.

But while the zoom lens detail drew me,
it was wildness appearing in my
small suburban wood I felt more deeply.

These were animals from books or TV,
radically misplaced, and shocking now with
their stark otherness and their eyeing of me

without concern. I stared back gauchely;
the same disbelieving staring that a
film-star pausing in the street might see.

The roebuck nonchalantly broke the spell.
The female stayed, but wanting to free her
I slid my foot, and she walked off as well.

Announcement

Someone near
you now has Chlamydia.

Startled, I look around, just the
flowing river and green countryside.

I realise the voice has spoken from the
trouser pocket where I keep my phone.

Closing social media I commit to tidying my
browsing, pressing lock more often than I do.

I resolve to cut down on sending others
muffled footsteps from the supermarket.

As for public service broadcasting,
I decide to stop before I'm giving

sexual health advice to the
queue in Waitrose.

Brionnfhionn

I walked beside wide fast water,
in a low place where provision
is received when given,
not sought and caught by human will.

I was far down in reverie
when a salmon leapt three men high,
hung while the world and I
moved still and silent under it.

The salmon's arc of fall was clear;
my arms rose in place of river
and thrilling live silver
landed stagger-heavy in them.

I pulled the fish against my chest;
as long as a man's striding tread
and deeper than his head,
all over, brief rainbows dripping.

I knelt, its weight across my thighs,
gills failing in the too thin air,
the golden round-eyed stare
an invitation beckoning.

I wasn't wise enough to know
the wisdom I was being shown,
I let the salmon down,
down in the quick river's running.

Debris

The river's dropped its level overnight
and like an ebbing tide left a washed-flat
arc of beach, but tiny, a cliff-backed
cove in miniature, a childhood's delight.
Look, bobbing in towards the beach a small
red speed-boat crewed by a rat and hamster.
Oh! Wasp-waisted Barbie's on her lounger,
Ken's stiff-limbed climbing up the sheer cliff wall.

Debris of all sorts on these little beaches,
sticks, leaves, bits of rope, tangled on the shore.
And oddments that I recognise too well:
the Rorschach of the landscape catches
debris of my own, stuff I might ignore
when it’s half-submerged and hidden by the swell.

Stepping stones

Where it's wide, stepping stones cross the river.
Thirty-eight, but none cared for; some sinking,
others sliding, I doubt I'd get over
now without wet feet or a full soaking.
I crossed them once, years ago; went with care,
watching each footstep land, but fast, driven
by some sense I'd topple in if I dare
slow down and lose my forward motion.

But on the centre stone I stopped, turned upstream;
a great plain of mirrored autumn colour,
vast to my smallness, was coming downstream
towards me. The delight of something never
seen before caught me, and standing out there,
so exposed, I felt a thrill of small fear.

Fish

The sound of a kiss, a sloppy wet one,
but only ripples when I look across;
a brown trout or grayling taking a fallen
fly from the river's glassy surface.
Upstream I see a fisherman refresh
his lure, start again the to and fro
of rod and snaking cast. *Stay here fish,*
on my still stretch, I'll watch over you.

I used to fish though, was ten when I first
persuaded one to take my feathered hook.
The tackle's breaking strain was twice his weight,
I hauled him out, hit him on a rock.
I'd held him live a while, but there was no line
I had to draw and hold to, he was mine.

Unseen

Beside my stone seat the branch of an ash
is horizontal above the river.
Along it, small trees, pushing up through moss,
are fractalled to the height of a finger;
a shrunken woodland that's a miniature
of mine. I pause. So, is my own landscape
a small copy? But in some way too obscure
for me to grasp, wanting form and shape.

I'm engaged now and drawn to wondering
if my sense of more than water, rocks, trees, birds
begs the question of an unseen holding,
a framing scheme for which I've no words.
Above me, the coy swept limbs of larches
hold small black cones on blue, ellipses.

Curlew

My eyes drawn by the flight of a bird;
mottled browns and a crescent bill slung
under balancing, gliding wings, wind-hung
over the sheep-green hill, and my heart lured
onto open ground. Exposed, defenceless,
I take the full hit of the calling:
an intravenous rush of pure longing
shocking my soft heart and veins breathless.

First pleading, then urgent and quickening
a rising trilled piping. Repeat and restart
until the notes slow, lose their tight shrillness.
Softening now, a hesitant burbling
para-glides down with the bird and my heart
echoing, calms to a gentling stillness.

Starlings

Consciousness appears inside a glove of birds,
a mime's hand delighting in its fluid
easy exploration of space and time.
The hand gestures, high and wide, expansive,
then rolls and closes in upon itself;
a tightened fist of close packed birds dropping
with the weight of thousands until it spreads
and lifts itself just feet above the ground.

Now there are two gloved hands. They briefly touch,
mirrored before they merge; the paired mime's hands
become huge wings and consciousness at play
holds up the swirling flock as if one bird.
It swarms again, surges, pauses, then rains down,
shades of dark pouring from the evening sky.

Donkeys

On Bridlington beach on a summerless day in July,
kids in cagoules over swim suits, windbreaks tacking to port.
A smiley face kite is rising and dipping, fighting Captain Dad
who's intent on control in his camouflage knee-length shorts,
that turn now and then into grey fifties turn-ups with pleats.

On flattened wet sand out to sea-ward a small boy is working
with Panamanian vision, digging to bring an ocean to the moat
of his castle. And harnessed in line abreast, back-siding
into the wind, four donkeys stand facing their handler
who's down on a stool passing up carrots and fruit.

I'm again on my one donkey ride as a child, hands clutching
the mane of a nameless stead, jogged off the saddle,
left flat on the trotting donkey's back. *Sit up, sit up,* shout two
twenty-somethings from distance, but I can't, and watch the wet,
hard, sea-soaked finger prints of the beach fly by under me.

No devilish donkeys today, just cuddly brown burros
patiently waiting their turn for a piece of banana.
Paddy and Tyson and Titch have names on brass plaques on
their foreheads but not, I can see, that fourth one out on the end.
I direct a severe squint at: 'The Donkey with no name'.

Ennio Morricone's music plays loudly. I roll an imagined
cheroot from one side of my mouth to the other.
The donkey watches, does the same with a piece of banana.
In the Hollywood distance, beach becomes desert
and two twenty-somethings turn into cowboy film cacti.

I ask the team handler the unnamed one's name.
From her stool she ignores me, then without turning says, *Nosey*.
I walk away thoughtful, unclear if this is the answer
I sought or a passive-aggressive response to my question.
Leaving the beach I sense more *hey!* than *ho* in donkey riding.

Up on the prom a breeze carries smells of deep frying do-nuts,
cracks open a flag overhead. Two lock-ups sell buckets and spades,
beach balls and frisbees, pink stetsons and kiss-me-quick hats;
wide-eyed caves of luminous treasure, day-glo that fades
the beige of the beach and the shirt collar grey of the sky.

Moving mountains

Tomorrow, she will move Ben Nevis.
    She will. She's found him on a web-site,
        the one that offers friendship without charge.

She's phoned Ben, talked for ages, he's keen.
    She's booked on the early train to Glasgow,
        they're meeting next to Burns in George Square.

The local news is sending a reporter.
    The man there laughed and got excited
        when she told him that her name is Faith.

The DNA of Highland driving

It surprises me how exhilarating it is, driving on this
dipping, rising road, adjusting my speed for these
long, easy curves, smiling at the rightness of my line.

I'm guessing this thrill's from somewhere deep in me,
or even deeper, from self I wouldn't recognise as me.
I grand prix the car through a left hand bend, feel the

pounding arc of a predator closing on running prey,
I'm fastened in my seat but lean with the hunter's
curving pursuit. Now a right hand, fast, downhill,

the stooping arc of a peregrine, speeding hard on a
wheeling line before shattering a pigeon's bones.
It could be I'm a child again, playing at fighter planes,

but these games are from a basement place where
not-ready-to-get-rid stuff is stored, a function of old
DNA, developed continents ago in the cause of gene

survival and my inheritance. I glance left suddenly,
my peripheral vision has caught two deer standing
by a stream, still, heads high, alert to everything.

Croig harbour

Imagine BC is Before
CalMac, so that in some
century BC,

in a different time,
another society,
cattle are being landed

on Croig's small stone jetty,
brought across in open
sailing boats from Coll,

Tiree, packed close, two,
three, a dozen at a time,
boats, sails lowered, hauled in

the final stretch on ropes,
men shouting orders, oaths,
cattle crying, slipping

on each other's fear and
dripping with it, men and
cattle clambering to the

quay with unsteady legs,
directions yelled, sticks
raised and landed, bellowing,

the sour sweet smell
        of cattle trudging past,
                lowing their way through Mull,

swum and driven south to
        pole-axes in Glasgow,
                Edinburgh, London.

Note: CalMac is the commonly used name for Caledonian MacBrayne, the company which since 1851 has operated most of the ferries that run connections between the Hebridean islands and between the islands and the mainland.

Landings

I smash off limpets with a fist sized lump
of rock, hook out their insides for crabbing.
She's watching me, uncertain; I see I might,
for the first time with her, have become a killer.

Dropping the weighted and now baited hook
in shallow water left beside the quay
I hand her the line, hope this may count as bail.
I step back, gaze at gulls, sea, lobster creels.

I've got one! I've got one! Her arm out straight,
a small crab hanging stubborn on the line.
You leave some for me now, says a man who
winks at me and opens the harbour store.

A truck is beeping backing down the track,
he takes a trolley load of crates to meet it.
She and I peer in at scrambling, crawling
sea things; strange crabs, I ask him what they are.

Velvet Swimming crabs, he says, *landing loads*
here now. They're going south, down to Spain.
What for? she asks. He laughs. I tell her:
they eat these there, cook them first of course.

We walk back to her bucket and the crab.
I ask if I should tip it in. *No,* she says, *I will.*
She takes the plastic bucket, kneels down where
the quayside's low, and gently slides him in.

Snap

And this one, I say, *look, you and me sitting*
on those old rocks at the far end of the island.

The oldest rocks in the country, I've read,
worn down but still features in the landscape,
and him, ten, next to me in perfect mirroring;
expression, gestures, all matching: the angled head,
the sceptic's gaze, the forearm resting on a knee.

He's staring at the image: I wonder how he sees
his younger self, and how he sees that man
beside him who back then was his age now.

I remember finding old photos of my father,
wincing as the photos turned to mirrors,
and I wondered what my father would have
made of his own hand-me-down deja vu.
I'd assumed each generation began again.

Do you remember those rocks? I ask him.

So old and worn but so deep seated, lasting;
like they've always been there, always will be.

Time, please

Bringing beers like you're taking an exam
you sit down next to me. I can see how
years are passing, even sitting you're now
at least a forehead taller than I am.

Lifting up your man-sized glass you say *cheers*
before sipping from it, but in a way
that's exaggerated, using cliché
to both hide and demonstrate we're not peers.

I pick up my own beer, pause to embrace
the rite of passage, say *thank you.* I smile
as a log flares and shifts in the fireplace.

Events get buried by events, I'll file
away a memory of today in case;
for a while we overlap, just a while.